The Manager's Guide to Employee Feedback

Master this essential management skill and boost your
team's performance

Glenn Devey

The Manager's Guide to Employee Feedback

First published: January 2014

Production Reference: 2100114

Published by Impackt Publishing Ltd.
Livery Place
35 Livery Street
Birmingham B3 2PB, UK.

ISBN 978-1-78300-000-5

www.Impacktpub.com

Cover Image by Jarek Blaminsky (milak6@wp.pl)

Credits

Author
Glenn Devey

Reviewers
Kath Akoslovski
James Border
Andy Ibbitson

Project Coordinators
Anurag Banerjee
Priyanka Goel

Technical Editor
Jalasha D'costa

Copy Editors
Jalasha D'costa
Maria Gould
Paul Hindle

Graphics
Ronak Dhruv

Proofreaders
Maria Gould
Paul Hindle

Cover Work
Melwyn D'sa

Production Coordinator
Melwyn D'sa

Commissioning Editors
Stephanie Moss
Danielle Rosen

Foreword

It was back in the early 1980s that Kenneth Blanchard and Spencer Johnson in their book, *The One Minute Manager*, described feedback as "The Breakfast of Champions". Delivered well with care and positive intent, feedback can inspire us and help us access our full potential. Many of us, however, will be able to cite experiences of feedback (both delivered and received) when the impact has not been motivational.

Creating the environment and readiness for effective communication in the workplace is a critical leadership skill for people, whatever role they perform. For a team to achieve optimal performance, all members of the team carry the responsibility to hold themselves and each other to account for fulfilling their role. Being able to deliver strong messages of support and of expectation with clarity and respect for colleagues is a skill to be developed and nurtured for all aspiring leaders.

Glenn Devey presents a range of strategies to help us in this development. His engaging style, his authentic appreciation of the challenges this presents, and his enthusiastic encouragement to us all make this book a very accessible and enjoyable read.

He draws on his own experiences with a refreshing honesty, and his highly developed coaching and mentoring skills are in evidence as he encourages us to think for ourselves and work things out through experience as opposed to calling on us to simply take his word for it.

Looking back at my own experiences in managing and leading others, I recognize that I would have benefitted from knowing the techniques and approaches Glenn explores. Glenn's prompts for good practices have been a very helpful reminder for me, and I'm sure they will be helpful ideas for everyone working and interacting with others.

Mike Hurley
Director of Intuition Discovery and Development Ltd.
September 2013

About the Author

Glenn Devey currently works as a management consultant building on an industrial career spanning almost 30 years. After beginning his career in the Telecoms industry, he moved into the Automotive industry where he spent 17 years working in Engineering Management leading small and large teams of engineers working on complex new products. He resigned his corporate position in 2007 to work freelance as a trainer, coach, and consultant following a passion for personal and professional development. Since then, his career has taken him across both the public and private sector working to train the next generation of new managers and also working as an executive coach to experienced and senior leaders in business. Glenn holds recognized qualifications in coaching, mentoring, training, NLP, Six Sigma, and at the time of writing, is studying for an MBA. He has filed a successful patent, holds a Second Dan Black Belt in Karate, and also plays electric bass with a local Blues band.

You can join Glenn and the growing Feedback community here `https://www.facebook.com/GuideToGivingFeedback` or you can connect with Glenn personally at `http://www.linkedin.com/in/glenndevey`

I'd like to thank the following people who have inspired me to write this book: Sandra Goddard, my first coach, who really stretched my thinking. Peter Hill, for his teaching and supervision work with me as a developing coach. Mike Hurley, my mentor, who took me under his wing and taught me about coaching and the coaching industry.

Ellen Bothwick, my first NLP trainer, who saw something within me and gave me the opportunity to work within the industry. David Shephard, Ralph Watson, and David Smallwood, who are all fantastic NLP trainers with outstanding feedback skills.

Finally, my two beautiful daughters, Annabelle and Imogen, who have taught me more about human behavior than I sometimes wanted to know.

About the Reviewers

Kath Akoslovski has over 28 years' experience of working as a senior manager with a diverse range of organizations across the UK. She is also a Master Practitioner in Neuro-Linguistic Programming (NLP), accredited coach, and trainer.

Kath established Bridge2succeed Ltd. 15 years ago and is very successful in developing work relationships at a senior decision-making level to build long term business partnerships. She operates as a key driver of organizational change and development through people, systems, and processes. Through her natural ability to develop rapport quickly with people at all levels, she is able to achieve results by gaining the collaboration of staff. As an interim manager, she has been successful in transforming areas of deficit and poor performance into successful productive happy work areas.

Kath is passionate about developing people to their full potential through coaching teams and individuals. She believes that everyone has a 'gift' / natural talent and through effective communications, nurturing and support will bring this to the fore. The long term benefits to the individual and organization is invaluable. For more information about Kath, visit www.bridge2succeed.co.uk and www.mindfit.org.uk.

James Border started his career as an engineer in the Aerospace industry before moving into Automotive, where he formed the opinion that to have a greater influence on the finished product required a move into project management. A move to the power industry gave him the opportunity to manage diverse global teams and therefore led to the development of team-oriented skills. So, being invited to contribute to this book about providing feedback was a natural and relevant progression.

Andy Ibbitson is a business improvement specialist who has operated in the Construction, Infrastructure, Automotive, Healthcare, and Manufacturing sectors. With a Master of Science degree in Automotive Component Manufacturing and an MBA in Engineering Management, Andy began his career in the UK construction industry, where his engineering and manufacturing skills were first developed. His formative years were at Jaguar Land Rover in the UK, where he delivered in a number of senior roles over a course of 20 years and his lean skills and coaching knowledge were embedded. After leaving JLR, he ventured into the NHS, the UK healthcare system, where he undertook a senior role as a Service Improvement Officer. After achieving much in the NHS, Andy moved back into the Construction sector where he led and directed a number of successful interventions working on the UK highways network and infrastructure framework for Carillion as Business Improvement Director.

Andy took up the challenge to venture in to the Asia Pacific region in July 2011, where he has delivered on a number of Business Improvement assignments and now works for BGC Contracting in Western Australia. Andy is a passionate coach who believes in the power of simple but effective engagement tools to deliver consistent performance in organizations.

Andy's current role is National Business Improvement Manager with BGC Contracting in Western Australia.

Andy has worked as an Executive Editor on *The Lean Information Management Toolkit*, a book written by *Robin Smith*.

I would like to thank Glenn Devey. He's a great coach and I wish him all the best in his career.

Contents

Preface

Q. What is the shortest word in the English language that contains the letters a, b, c, d, e, and f?

A. Feedback.

My feedback journey

I clearly remember the first time that I was introduced to the concept of feedback; it was in an Electronics lesson, rather strangely. The class lecturer stood at the blackboard with a piece of chalk (as they did in the last century) and drew the following diagram:

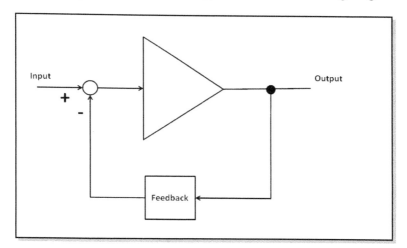

He then made a rather bold claim about the meaning of feedback:

> *"Taking a portion of the output and comparing it with the input to decide whether you are getting what you want out of a system."*

And in a beautifully simple way, he gave me a definition that has stayed with me for over 25 years.

I'd had report cards throughout my school life, but it wasn't really until I was about age 21 and at the start of my professional career that I had my first piece of performance feedback. You'll read about it later in *Chapter 3, Addressing Specific Performance Issues*, but it wasn't really very helpful. From there, I had mixed experiences with managers that I worked for; some spent time and effort in developing their staff and would discuss objectives clearly and take the time to give feedback in the best way that they could. Others were less precise and articulate.

So, when I was given my first management opportunity at age 30 back in 2000, I had a broad spectrum of experiences from which to draw on and formulate my feedback skills. My first few years as a manager were quite a rollercoaster; the manager who recruited me left the department one week after I was promoted, and I was left without any supervision for three months. I remember the Head of Department, Jeff, sitting me down in his office and asking me how I was getting on. I told him that it was tough, but I was enjoying it. He smiled a wry smile and looked away out of the window as he spoke; he told me that being a line manager was a draughty position—you sometimes get it in the neck from above and below!

In 2007, I resigned from my corporate position to work freelance as a management trainer and coach. I undertook a lot of personal and professional development around this time and learned more about linguistics and raising performance in others. Hungry for more, I searched Amazon for books about feedback, but I was disappointed by the number of titles available on the topic. The topic cropped up from time to time on training courses, mainly when I was training new managers or internal coaches, and I began to build up a mental collection of ideas, models, and theories about how to give feedback in a number of different situations and contexts. I soon realized that there wasn't a universal feedback model, but there were some common principles that could be applied irrespective of the situation you were in. I resolved to one day write a book on giving feedback, to bring together all of my learning and practice into one concise guide. I particularly wanted it to be of use to newly promoted managers, to spare them some of the mistakes and pitfalls that I had made along the way. I think it was Winston Churchill who once said "I'm always ready to learn, but I don't always enjoy being taught!"

So here you have it, a collection of personal learning gathered over a 25 year span inside large corporations and also from operating as a freelance consultant. Most of these lessons were learned the hard way, and in some respects, they stick firmer because of that.

I sincerely hope that you are ready to learn, and also that you enjoy being taught.

What this book covers

Chapter 1, Feedback Fundamentals, describes the seven key principles that underpin the concept of delivering feedback that is useful and actionable to your staff.

Chapter 2, Delivering Balanced Feedback, introduces the WIN model of feedback, which can be used to deliver balanced feedback in performance conversations such as one-to-one reviews, appraisals, and after a key event in the workplace.

Chapter 3, Addressing Specific Performance Issues, details the BAR feedback model for use after a specific incident in the workplace that requires reflection and a re-enforcement or change in behavior.

Chapter 4, Delivering a Reprimand, discusses Bowers and Bowers' DESC model of feedback, for use in correctional conversations.

Chapter 5, Giving Feedback to Colleagues and Managers, offers strategies for feeding upwards in a hierarchy, disagreeing eloquently, and subtle influencing techniques.

Chapter 6, Integrating Your New Skills, suggests a game plan for developing your new skills and lists some ways of managing your state to improve your delivery.

Who this book is for

This book is a terrific resource for newly hired or promoted managers who wish to start their career equipped with excellent conversational feedback skills. It will also be invaluable to experienced managers who want to develop better strategies for helping employees raise their performance at work. Ambitious individuals wishing to enhance their career prospects by becoming familiar with fundamental management skills will also be at an advantage over other candidates after integrating these skills.

Conventions

In this book, you will find a number of styles of text that distinguish between different kinds of information. Here are some examples of these styles, and an explanation of their meaning.

New terms and **important words** are shown in bold.

Make a Note
Warnings or important notes appear in a box like this.

Tip
Tips and tricks appear like this.

Action Point
Action points appear like this

Reader feedback

Feedback from our readers is always welcome. Let us know what you think about this book—what you liked or may have disliked. Reader feedback is important for us to develop titles that you really get the most out of.

To send us general feedback, simply send an e-mail to `feedback@impacktpublishing.com`, and mention the book title via the subject of your message.

If there is a book that you need and would like to see us publish, please send us a note via the **SUGGEST A TITLE** form on `www.impacktpublishing.com`, or send an e-mail to `suggest@impacktpublishing.com`.

If there is a topic that you have expertise in and you are interested in either writing or contributing to a book, see our author guide on `www.impacktpublishing.com/authors`.

Customer support

Now that you are the proud owner of an Impackt book, we have a number of things to help you to get the most from your purchase.

Piracy

Piracy of copyright material on the Internet is an ongoing problem across all media. At Packt, we take the protection of our copyright and licenses very seriously. If you come across any illegal copies of our works, in any form, on the Internet, please provide us with the location address or website name immediately so that we can pursue a remedy.

Please contact us at `copyright@impacktpublishing.com` with a link to the suspected pirated material.

We appreciate your help in protecting our authors, and our ability to bring you valuable content.

Questions

You can contact us at `questions@impacktpublishing.com` if you are having a problem with any aspect of the book, and we will do our best to address it.

Feedback Fundamentals

"Techniques are many, principles are few. Techniques vary, principles never do."

—(Source unknown)

The purpose of this chapter is to give you some guiding principles that you can apply right away when you need to deliver feedback. This is most likely a new area for you to explore as a recently promoted manager; you have probably had feedback yourself with varying degrees of quality, but now is the time for you to start to deliver your own feedback messages to your staff. Typical examples could be:

➤ Commenting on the quality of a finished piece of work

➤ Assessing someone's overall results at the end of an operational quarter

➤ Helping someone improve their leadership behaviors at work

➤ Correcting someone who isn't adhering to organizational policy

In this chapter, you will learn how to deliver feedback using the following principles within EARSHOT:

➤ Evidence-based

➤ Activity-focused

➤ Results-orientated

➤ Specific

➤ Honesty

➤ Only positive language

➤ Timed well

Start now!

As a newly promoted or hired manager, your staff, peers, and upper management will be observing your behavior and results in the workplace. People will want to understand how you operate and what your expectations are. From your staff's perspective, this will range from "How can I please my boss and exceed my objectives?", all the way down to "How little can I get away with?". Your peers will be wondering whether they can rely on you, whether you can be trusted, or whether you will attempt to show them up. Your upper management will likely just have one question in mind:

"Are you going to deliver?"

So, if you are going to make a purposeful change in your behavior and improve your results by reading this book, then the best time to make that change is *now*. Change is never easier than in the present moment. The longer you delay it, the more reasons or anxiety will develop in your mind that will prevent it from happening. And from your staff's perspective, the more they get used to their new manager's style, the harder it will be for them to accept a change in it. If you don't believe me, try this exercise:

1. Tell your staff that they can finish half an hour earlier each day, for the same pay.
2. Three months later, tell them that they have to go back to how it was before.
3. Consult with HR on how to quickly recruit a replacement team.

Secondly, you have a duty and responsibility as a manager to ensure that your staff hit their targets and also develop professionally along the way. If you don't provide effective feedback, you have no one but yourself to blame if your staff don't perform.

Aside from all of the hard work that you put in to get yourself to this stage in your career, I'll bet there was someone who invested their time, experience, and wisdom in you. Do the right thing and pay it forwards by giving your staff feedback that helps them be the best that they can be in the workplace.

Where are you now?

For anyone whose life has been enriched by the invention of SatNav (shorter journeys, lower blood pressure, and better composure), you will appreciate the importance of entering your starting postal or zip code. In the context of giving your first critical feedback to an employee, take a few of those reclaimed SatNav moments to establish your starting point by answering true or false to the following questions about delivering feedback. It's important that you do this so you can establish your current level of feedback skill and assess where you need to develop the most:

1. Feedback is best delivered sometime after the event it concerns, allowing plenty of time for planning. (True/False)
2. Attitude, motivation, and commitment are key focus areas for feedback. (True/False)
3. Evidence, results, and customer feedback are essentials for good feedback. (True/False)
4. Delivering someone else's feedback message or opinion about an event you haven't witnessed is to be avoided where possible. (True/False)

5. Saying "Don't swear and shout in the office" is effective feedback. (True/False)

6. If properly constructed, feedback can be delivered publicly or in a group. (True/False)

7. A manager's opinion is more valuable than evidence-based feedback. (True/False)

8. Clearly explaining to staff what good performance looks and sounds like is key to increased performance and output. (True/False)

9. Referencing a specific situation is more effective than speaking generally about the previous three months. (True/False)

10. You must use one of the feedback models exactly as listed in this book. (True/False)

Make a Note

The answers are in the Appendix, and a similar test will be repeated at the end of the book as evidence of your expanded skills base.

Evidence based

1. Delivering good feedback is both an art and a science. The way that you choose your words, how you pace your delivery in terms of emphasis and pauses... all contribute toward a conversation that feels natural and is part of your own conversational style. In conjunction with the principles and models that you're going to learn here, this section addresses the art of giving feedback. The content, however, is where the science part fits in. Like any good scientific endeavor, it is evidence-based.

Recall for a moment a time when you may have been given some feedback that was:

➤ Inaccurate

➤ Largely opinion-based

➤ Contained hearsay

Did you take it on board and modify your own behavior? Opinions have their place, but in my opinion, only when you ask for the experience of the person giving it. Walk into any bar on a Saturday afternoon and you'll hear many opinions about how sport, politics, or religion should be run, usually by people unqualified to make the statements!

So, the next two principles are going to guide you through crafting evidence-based feedback.

Activity focused

Working with someone's activity—what they have actually done—is one of the most powerful approaches you can take as a manager. In fact, it's the only approach to take. While you may become tempted to fulfill other roles—counselor, consultant, or clairvoyant—observing, recording, and feeding back about what was actually done or not done will leverage the largest change in your team's performance and results.

Here are a few examples of behavioral versus non-behavioral observations:

"I noticed that during the team meeting on Thursday, you raised the volume of your voice when James questioned you about your proposal." (Behavior)

"I think you got angry with James in the team meeting last week." (Mind reading)

"Sarah's met 8 out of 11 of her yearly targets, although I haven't seen her display enough of the "Drive for Results" behavior as written in our competency framework." (Behavior)

"I don't see manager potential in Rob; I don't think he wants the role enough." (Mind reading)

To focus exclusively on behavior isn't always an easy task, but it's worth the extra effort. The key to it is relying on your external senses and switching off your internal senses in the short term.

Make a Note

Anything you see, hear, or read in the first person will usually indicate a behavior. Anything you feel, think, mind read, or imagine won't be helpful.

Take a look at the following table:

Use	Avoid
I noticed	I think
I saw	I feel
I heard	My gut tells me
I watched	Intuitively
I listened	I just know

Don't get me wrong, all of the things in the right-hand column have a place in business and management, they just don't serve you well when you're developing your feedback skills. Put your opinions on ice unless someone specifically asks for them because your previous experience is going to add value to the situation.

A useful skill to develop is the use of verbatim—replaying back things that have been said, but striving to do it word for word without any interpretation. When you need to remind someone of a conversation, then repeating it verbatim is an example of taking a behavioral approach to language.

Action Point

What were the key behaviors that helped you get promoted or hired that you may wish to look out for in your staff? Note them down in the following space without saying "my attitude". Focus on things that you did, said, or carried out in specific, concrete, and measureable terms.

Results oriented

One of the paradigms to get your head around sooner rather than later as a new manager is that the people above you will generally assess you in terms of results, whereas the people who work for you will often want to talk about the effort they have put in or what they intended to do.

The road to Hell is littered with good intentions!

Organizations stand or fall based on their results. Therefore, it makes good sense to base your feedback discussions around what was delivered, finished, achieved, or accomplished. Depending on whether you work in the public or private sector, military or third sector, or anywhere else, examples of this could be:

> ➤ Sales revenue
> ➤ Profit
> ➤ New business enquiries or orders
> ➤ Pages written
> ➤ Money saved
> ➤ Goals scored
> ➤ Queries resolved

The preceding list is a quantitative list—things that can be objectively measured in terms of quantity or numbers, as opposed to qualitative—subjectively assessed in terms of their "goodness or badness".

Straight away, you should see the value in taking this approach to giving feedback—it's simply not up for debate, as the numbers don't lie. And done in this way, you are continually focusing your staff's attention on improving the results of the organization—a strategy that your upper management will thank you for.

Action Point

How is success measured in your organization?

Take a moment to note down the objective measures by which your staff's performance is measured: numbers, dates, amounts, and so on. Use these in your feedback conversations.

Specific

Our third principle nicely complements the previous two, although it's more of a guide to how to construct your feedback as opposed to what to include in it. Being specific means that you use detailed, concise words and phrases as opposed to generalized, abstract descriptions. If you followed the previous section and used activity and results, that's great. This rule is about being as precise as possible when you are giving feedback and throughout the conversation. If you follow this rule:

> ➤ The receiver will be less inclined to dispute or refuse the observation, as your observation will be more closely aligned with their recollection

> ➤ It becomes easier to discuss what needs to happen instead of debating what did happen

> ➤ You will earn more respect from your new team as they'll perceive you as highly observant

> ➤ Staff will quickly learn what you expect from them when you articulate it regularly

Here are examples of generalizations to avoid and examples of specifics to use:

Generalizations	Specifics
It went well	You achieved the weekly target
Always	I've noticed on three occasions
Every time I ask you	Today when I asked you
You never do that	The last time I asked you, you didn't

Wherever you can, describe exactly what you witnessed with your external senses. So, speak about what you saw, what you heard, or what you read, not what you thought or felt at this stage. There is a time and a place for thoughts and feelings, but it isn't when you are describing behavior. Imagine that you are an officer of the law preparing a case, and what you say will be read out in court and dissected by a lawyer obsessed with linguistics.

Honesty

Honesty and **judgment** are two extremely valuable traits that you need to possess as you develop your style of management. With that said, one of those needs to be tempered when giving feedback and the other needs to be ruthlessly released.

You can't have too much honesty in business. Most CEOs would love to know exactly what's going on at an operational level, how their staff feel about the senior leadership team, what their customers think of them, and so on. But how often is that level of honesty used? Many times I've seen someone in another team underperform throughout the year only to be completely destroyed by an end of year appraisal that they didn't expect to go so badly.

Fill in the following matrix with examples of managers you have worked with in the past or even who you work with now:

Very honest, not well respected	Very honest, very well respected
Not very honest, not well respected	Not very honest, very well respected

You probably noticed a link between people who are honest and who are respected. You can also conclude that as managers, they get good results. So, if a member of staff underperforms or needs to receive some feedback, for everyone's sake, take a deep breath and get on with it, however uncomfortable it may be. In my experience, a difficult conversation is a bit like a toothache; it rarely goes away on its own.

Given that this section is about the use of judgment, we'd better address that topic too. What I mean by judgment in this context is passing a verdict on someone—summing up their total and entire worth using a few all-encompassing words.

Examples of this would be words like:

- ➤ Good
- ➤ Bad
- ➤ Great
- ➤ Poor
- ➤ Excellent
- ➤ Atrocious

While the positive words here are nice to deliver and nice to hear, using any of the preceding has a fundamental drawback—how on earth do you act on them? Whether you are remarking on performance that should be repeated or changed, the preceding words are too vague for the receiver to internalize and either change or repeat.

Their use, I suspect, harks back to childhood tellings-off by parents or teachers; after all, being told that something was "atrocious" is pretty powerful. With that said, as adults in the workplace, we can provide more useful and actionable words for improvement.

Examples of judgmental feedback include:

> *"Your timekeeping is awful; you're a bad example to the new starters in the team."*

> *"That last report you wrote was utter rubbish. It was boring, messy, and rambling."*

> *"You have performed very poorly this quarter. You're an embarrassment to the department."*

Examples of non-judgmental feedback include:

> *"You've been late on three occasions this week."*

> *"Your figures in the previous report had two errors that would have given an inaccurate picture of the business this quarter. I was annoyed that I spotted them and you didn't."*

> *"Despite the one-to-one time that you and I have invested this month, you didn't meet all of the objectives that we agreed. I'm disappointed with that."*

You may notice that I've included some emotive words in the last two examples to explain how I'm feeling. This is not casting a judgment or putting a label on the receiver because the words are about how I'm feeling. In this way, I can be honest about performance and how I feel about it without saying things to damage someone's self-esteem.

It's a subtle difference, so here are some examples to make it explicit:

> *"I feel disappointed."* *(About my feelings)*

> *"You are a disappointment."* *(Judging or labeling someone)*

> *"I feel embarrassed by the results that we are discussing right now."* *(About me)*

> *"You're embarrassing."* *(Giving them a label or a judgment)*

Feelings are extremely powerful tools, so use them wisely and own your feeling statements; feedback, after all, is about improvement, not injury.

Only positive language

Believe it or not, I first came across this principle as a new parent reading a book about how to bring up happy and confident children. The book suggested that the majority of human behavior is driven from the unconscious mind; this means you don't always have to think about something consciously in order to perform an action. For example, things like tying your shoelaces or brushing your teeth are unconscious actions; you don't need to consciously think about each discrete step to perform the whole sequence. These are what we refer to as **habits** or **learned behaviors**. Interestingly, the unconscious mind doesn't seem to respond too well to the concept of negatives; do this quick exercise now in order to illustrate the point:

Make a Note

For the next five seconds, DO NOT think about a blue tree.

Pretty tough isn't it?

You have to think about it in order not to think about it. My guess is that you either saw a picture of a blue tree in your mind or repeated the words "blue tree" in your head.

Put another way, when a tightrope artist crosses the high wire, do you think they visualize themselves not falling to the ground and becoming Paper Mache, or do you think they visualize themselves crossing the wire successfully with poise, calmness, and balance? Positive thoughts, sounds, and images about what to do are much more useful than what not to do when giving human beings instructions.

Subsequently, my children have been raised with instructions such as:

➤ "Share nicely please"

➤ "Be gentle with your sister"

➤ "Take your plate to the kitchen please"

And with the exception of extremely messy bedrooms, the strategy has been a success. So, giving helpful and positive feedback in the workplace should consist of messages to re-enforce existing good practices, such as:

➤ "You used lots of color and images in that presentation; do more of that in your next one"

➤ "I noticed how you greeted those customers by shaking each of their hands and holding eye contact for a few seconds; carry on doing that"

➤ "Thanks for staying late to finish the Briggs report Anita, the MD saw and mentioned it"

Conversely, have you heard any of the following negative instructions given out in the workplace, or perhaps even received them yourself? Re-write them using only positive language that achieves the same end result (go on then, I'll do the first one for you):

➤ "Don't get nervous when you speak to…"

Becomes:

➤ "Just remain calm and composed when you speak to…"

Now try these yourself:

➤ "Don't forget to phone…"

➤ "Don't hesitate to get back to me…"

➤ "Don't get angry the next time…"

➤ "WET PAINT – DO NOT TOUCH" (we've all ignored that one!)

Now I'm not suggesting that the rules of good parenting apply directly to being an excellent manager (see what I did there?), but I have heard that being a manager is like running an adult day-care center sometimes

Timed well

There's an inverse relationship between time waited and feedback effectiveness: the quicker it's delivered after the event, the more effective it will be. Time has a way of distorting people's memory of events, so you should give feedback as soon after the actual event as possible. The only condition I'm going to put on this is to wait until you are in private if it's a piece of corrective feedback. The embarrassment generated by delivering corrective feedback in public only strengthens the will of the person to justify and defend what you say. Yes you can deliver good news and recognition in front of the whole team or department when merited, but the old saying, "praise loudly and blame softly" is a wise one.

Summary

In this chapter, you learned:

> ➤ How to use evidence of performance in your feedback delivery
> ➤ How to use tangible words that describe activity and behavior
> ➤ Ways of focusing on results in your conversations
> ➤ The art of being precise and exacting instead of something else
> ➤ The difference between honesty and judgment
> ➤ The importance of using positive language to create a blueprint for success
> ➤ When and where to deliver your message

If you read only this chapter out of the whole book and integrate all of the principles into your feedback skills, you would still be streets ahead of most other experienced managers. However, what follows is a collection of structures that will help you apply these principles until they are a habit.

Take a few moments to reflect now on what you've learned so far. Here's a couple of questions to assist you:

> ➤ Which principle stood out the most for you in this chapter?
> ➤ Which principle do you already apply well?
> ➤ Which one do you most need to integrate into your conversational skills as a new manager?

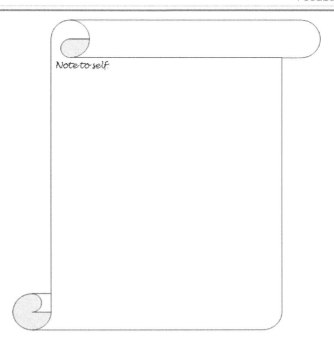

Note to self:

In the next chapter, I'll introduce you to the first structured model that you can easily learn and use when delivering balanced feedback about overall performance in a period. And you'll meet Brian, who gave me my first gray hairs as a newly promoted manager.

Read on, intrepid explorer.

>2

Delivering Balanced Feedback

"In the theatre, the actor is given immediate feedback."

—*Charles Keating*

In this chapter, I will demonstrate a general feedback model for regular use with your staff. You don't have to follow the exact framework given here, but you should consistently incorporate feedback into your routine as a new manager. Again, this model is just one way of applying the core principles of feedback, and the later chapters will detail models that are better suited to other, more specific situations.

In this chapter, you will:

> ➤ Meet Brian, who taught me more about management and leadership than anyone else

> ➤ Learn about a yearly feedback structure to help build high performing teams

> ➤ Learn how to use the WIN model of feedback

> ➤ Apply your new feedback skills when writing "grown-up" appraisals

Meet Brian

My second management assignment was to lead a team of technical designers who sat at computer terminals for most of the day, designing schematic networks for large complex engineering systems. Unusually, there was an opportunity for this almost "back office" team of technical people to become a leading group in the department, driving forward the technical aspects of the programs that we delivered. I was really looking forward to the move. I had only been in management for six months, but my new bosses wanted me to head up the team and really shake things up. I sat with the outgoing manager to discuss the team's current workload and to understand more about the personalities within the team. Then he delivered a crushing blow: he had agreed to bring Brian into the team.

Brian was a very experienced designer who had worked all over the world for some really large corporations and in some very exotic locations. He had been with this particular organization for some ten years or so, and he knew a lot about the industry. However, there were three immediate challenges:

1.   He was rather argumentative, and seldom admitted to being wrong.
2.   He made frequent mistakes in his work.
3.   He was prone to falling asleep at his desk.

Now number 1 I could cope with; a bit of spirited debate and technical conflict was in fact a good thing. Number 2 I was prepared to work with, but number 3 was a bit of a mystery. How on earth had this situation been allowed to carry on? It had become somewhat of a department joke, and it was down to me to fix it.

I could probably write an entire book on my management adventures with Brian, however at this stage, it's probably enough to state the conclusion that some of you will already have jumped to: Brian was not getting regular and actionable feedback about both his results and behavior at work. Boy was I about to shake things up!

We'll pick up the story with Brian again before the end of the chapter, but for now I'd like to share with you the structure that I have successfully and repeatedly used to give direction and feedback to my teams.

My management calendar

Fairly quickly, I settled into a routine of setting objectives and discussing how they were progressing with the team. For most of my management career, I managed fairly large, diverse teams with multiple project responsibilities. As a new manager, I soon learned that you need to know what each of your staff is working on and whether they are delivering on their commitments or not. In order to do this, I established a regular pattern of activity with my teams that I used for many years and which I still refer to now when I'm training new managers. This is the structure that I wrapped around my nocturnal nemesis:

Once per day

Speak to each of your staff, a mixture of work and social conversations. You'd be surprised how many managers don't do this even when they are in the office.

Once per week

Spend about 45 minutes with each of your staff (or as small project teams if appropriate) reviewing what they have done over the last week and what they need to accomplish over the coming weeks. Let them know whether they are on track or not, and if not, discuss what they can do to recover. Also, hold a whole team meeting to cascade business results, department changes, promotions, new hires, and other matters such as social events.

Once per month

Hold an hour long one-to-one discussion with each team member to coach, develop, and deliver feedback about their individual performance. Use the **WIN** model discussed in this chapter and invite feedback from your staff on how you are performing. Recommend that they buy this book.

Once per quarter

Individually discuss career aspirations with each of your team members. Take an interest in their aspirations, aims, and hopes for the future. If your organization promotes the use of Personal Development Plans or Career Maps, review them and encourage your staff to keep them up-to-date.

Twice per year

Deliver formal feedback and complete your company's prescribed appraisal and review process, document the discussion, and file it with Human Resources.

Obviously, depending on the size of your organization and its culture, some of this may not exist or may need to be changed or created as appropriate. But as an overall framework or structure, I hope you can see some advantages to starting off this way. As a new manager, you will want to start to develop your own style of operating, but in the absence of any ideas of how to go about that, this is a good place to start.

Back to Brian

If this structure had previously been followed and executed accurately, do you think that Brian's performance and results would have carried on in the pattern that they had done? I would argue not, and there would have been some change in his behavior. Of course, it's not necessary to turn every employee into the next head of department, and sadly there will be times when a capability or performance management approach has to be taken. Now, you might also think that this seems like a large and elaborate structure to solve a specific problem, and I would agree with you. However, the advantage of operating this way is that it gives you a "catch-all" approach to successfully leading a team and delivering on your promises. It also gives you a springboard to deliver at least twelve high-quality feedback discussions every year by using the WIN model once per month. I know people who probably haven't had twelve high-quality feedback discussions in their whole career!

The WIN model

> ➤ What went well
>
> ➤ Interesting aspects of performance
>
> ➤ Next time…

Let's take a look at the **WIN** model of feedback, which was derived from an Eastern European sports coaching model. It's a structure for emphasizing the positive aspects of someone's performance and also for suggesting areas of improvement. In that sense, it's a "balanced" model. Where some people have come unstuck using an approach like this is in trying to deliver a reprimand with it. If you need to have a purely corrective conversation with someone, use the DESC model in *Chapter 4*, *Delivering a Reprimand*. That model doesn't attempt to highlight positives at the same time!

What went well

Here's an opportunity to describe what someone has done that you want them to keep doing and, in fact, do more of. Of course, using the principles from *Chapter 1*, *Feedback Fundamentals*, you will ensure that they are within **EARSHOT**. You will need to evaluate your staff by both the end results that they deliver and also while they are "in flight" so to speak; going about their daily activities. In addition to any data reports you get about what they are delivering, shadow them in meetings that they attend and watch them as they speak to a customer or a group of colleagues. See how they go about their daily tasks and try to catch them doing something well! If you have the opportunity to solicit feedback from key customers or colleagues, then, done appropriately, this can prove to be a rich source of information from another perspective. Humans thrive on feedback and recognition, and positive acknowledgment works extremely well.

For example:

"You've delivered all three software specifications this month that we agreed on, and I noticed how many times you had to work outside core hours to do that. I appreciate that, and it has been commented on by my boss too."

"The presentation you gave to our prospective clients at the showcase used a really good case study about how we delivered a 20 percent cost reduction to Smith & Black. I'd encourage you to use something similar in the presentation you are currently writing."

"I see that the team's results from the last quarter are in, and sales figures are up by 11 percent on the same period last year. I'm really pleased about that. There's been a 31 percent increase in appointments made by the field sales team too, which has been instrumental in delivering that."

Interesting aspects of performance

This part of the model invites the receiver to reflect on a part of their performance and come to their own conclusions about how they have performed. You're going to work within EARSHOT still, but leave them to decide for themselves about whether it was a good thing or not.

For example:

> *"What was interesting about the way that you conducted the interview with Mary Evans was the way in which you asked her to describe what she wanted her boss to be saying to her at her year-end review; I've not heard that question used before, where did you learn it from?"*

> *"I was very intrigued by your approach to dealing with the irate customer who wrote and called us several times last week. You calmed them down within the first five minutes of taking the call by matching their voice tone and speed and then slowing them down gradually. How did you know it was time to take that approach?"*

> *"I'm curious about how you managed to attend and repair fourteen appliance call-outs in two days... most technicians will do ten at the most. Tell me more about that..."*

Next time...

This section allows you to highlight things that need to be changed, still within the EARSHOT principles. Of course, you may need to describe an event that happened that was undesirable, but the key is to give a positive instruction to be followed next time instead of just mandating "Don't do it again."

For example:

> *"Next time there's a threat of disruptive action by the students, I want you to bring it directly to my attention after you've alerted site security."*

> *"Next time you think you're not going to be able to meet an important client deadline, I want you to arrange for additional resources to be allocated to the task at least three days before it's due to be completed."*

> *"Next time that you are stuck for ideas on a print layout, why not ask Jenny to take a look at it and give you some of her ideas?"*

If you are new to both management and the WIN model, it may feel a little awkward the first time you run it through, which is perfectly natural. So, invest some time preparing for the conversation, but don't over-rehearse. There are a couple of things to bear in mind too: firstly, it is your responsibility and privilege to give feedback to staff, and secondly, you have earned the right to have this conversation due to your own performance and potential. Treat it like any other new skill, and anticipate that with time and practice it will become easier; which it will.

Time to practice

Now you're going to do an exercise to hone your new feedback skills. The WIN model can be applied to both verbal and written feedback, such as when writing an appraisal document.

Make a Note

If your organization uses a formal appraisal template, there will still probably be some space in which to write some free text about how you have assessed and perceived someone's performance over a period of time.

This is exactly what I did with Brian to begin the long and difficult task of changing his behavior and achievements over the coming months.

Take a sheet of A4 paper and divide the page up horizontally into three sections in which to write. The first one is for "W", the second for "I", and the last one for "N". Your task is to write a piece of feedback that you'd like to deliver to one of your team members using the WIN model. You can write these notes to be used in a face-to-face discussion or as typed notes to go into an end of year review. If you are going to use them in a written appraisal, pay special attention to the next section.

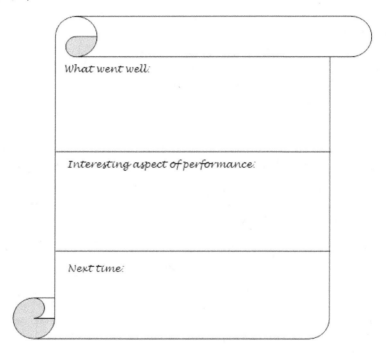

Grown-up appraisals

Appraisals in the workplace are not supposed to be written like school reports to be read by parents!

I physically cringe when I see a professional, grown-up appraisal written in the third person, like this:

"Dave has worked well to hit all of his targets this year..."

The appraisal is meant to stimulate a conversation between you and Dave, not to be read by Dave's Mum or Dad! It's not meant to be written for HR either; performance and results are owned by line management (yes, that's you now!), not anyone else. Please write in the first person!

"You have met or exceeded all of your targets this year…"

Back to Brian

I used this exact structure to deliver Brian's first piece of formal feedback not long after I took ownership of the team.

The initial result?

Brian went absolutely ballistic and told me that he had never heard such rubbish, and that he didn't know how I had been promoted to manager. He stormed out of the room and went home. He'd been allowed to continue with his patterns of behavior for such a long time that he had accepted them as normal.

However:

> ➤ My senior manager told me that he'd support me every step of the way
> ➤ My colleagues patted me on the back and told me it should have happened a long time ago

Start as you mean to go on in this new phase of your career. If you have any people like Brian in your team, please address them immediately, but remember that feedback can be painful for some. Stand your ground and work as hard as possible to keep to the principles illustrated in *Chapter 1, Feedback Fundamentals*. Data, facts, and evidence can still be uncomfortable to be presented with, but are much harder to argue with.

Summary

In this chapter, you've learned a valuable new feedback model:

> ➤ What went well
> ➤ Interesting aspects of performance
> ➤ Next time…

It's one that you can use all year round at regular intervals with your staff to let them know what to continue doing and what to change. I've shared the yearly structure that I have repeatedly used to build better performing teams and you've had the chance to practice your new skills by writing down a piece of feedback. You've also met Brian.

Use the following space to capture any reflections that you had while working through the chapter. As a prompt:

➤ What can you most readily apply from this chapter?

➤ When can you apply it?

➤ What skills have you realized that you need to develop while reading?

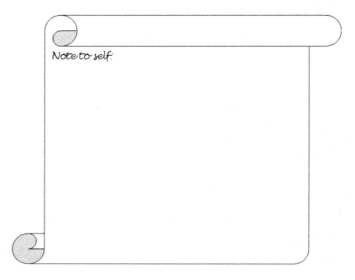

Note to self:

In the next chapter, you'll meet Kate, who gave me a piece of enduring but puzzling feedback. You'll also learn how to use the BAR feedback model in a more specific performance situation, and I'll share some perspectives that will help ease the more delicate feedback conversations.

3

Addressing Specific Performance Issues

"You can't blame people for doing stuff you didn't tell them they couldn't do."

—David Sandler

Having learned the general feedback principles and how to apply them throughout the year in *Chapter 2, Delivering Balanced Feedback*, you're now going to learn how to provide feedback based on a specific and instantaneous event; for example, an outcome or piece of behavior that you have observed in the workplace. Of course, timing will be extremely important in this feedback model, and put simply, it's a question of the sooner the better. Hopefully, you will be able to catch your staff doing great things around the office; in which case, this model can be used. But there will also be times when something didn't meet your expectations and needs to be corrected—and this is the context that we're going to focus on most in this chapter. In this case, you need to take the dentist's viewpoint: it's unlikely to get better on its own, so best get it dealt with as soon as possible.

In this chapter, you will:

> ➤ Meet Kate, who gave me a vague but lasting piece of feedback

> ➤ Learn how to apply the BAR feedback model

> ➤ Understand how to ease the delivery of critical feedback

> ➤ Be pleasantly surprised at how much you've learned already when you complete the short exercise at the end of the chapter!

Meet Kate

Back in 1990 when I was a mere 21-year old, I joined a large company in an Project Management role. The manager who recruited me took a sideways move three months after I joined, and I had a new line manager called Kate. The previous manager had known that I was new to the industry and had taken the time to guide and mentor me where necessary as I adjusted to the way things were done in the company. Kate, however, had a different way of managing. It was more of a "get on with it" style.

I've come across this style a few times over the years, and I'm sure you have too. If questioned about their approach to management, this style of manager will usually say something like:

> *"Look, you're all grownups, and I pay you $xx per year... I expect you to just do the job."*

This approach can work for experienced and motivated employees, but there are a few situations in which it won't work, and training a new hire is one of them.

As a new manager, you have many roles to get to grips with in your new job, including:

- ➤ Direction setter
- ➤ Decision maker
- ➤ Subject matter expert
- ➤ Role model
- ➤ Trainer
- ➤ Coach
- ➤ Mentor
- ➤ And of course, feedback giver

Sadly, the roles toward the bottom of the list sometimes get overlooked in favor of the ones toward the top. So, after a good start in my new company, I started to lose my way and felt abandoned in my new role. Kate didn't hold status reviews or give feedback and didn't always speak to me. After three months, it was time for the half yearly appraisals, at which time she wrote on my appraisal:

> *"Glenn seems to lack motivation in his work..."*

The truth of the matter was that Glenn didn't know what he was doing!

Strangely, that piece of feedback has stayed with me for a long time; it was never repeated in subsequent appraisals, and in fact the opposite became the norm for me.

There lies a fundamental problem with that piece of feedback. What on earth do you do with it once you've received it?

Of course, having read the previous chapters, you will know that managers need to hold regular status reviews as well as coaching and feedback sessions with their staff so that feedback becomes a regular and accepted part of the working calendar. But in addition to that, if someone is unable to relate a comment to a specific and recent experience, they are very unlikely to modify their behavior, which of course is the whole point of giving feedback in the first place. So, now let's take a look at the **BAR** model that can be used in relation to a specific incident that you need to address with someone.

The BAR model

➤ Background

➤ Activity

➤ Results

This model is ideal for first time managers as it's simple to remember and allows the conversation to flow naturally due to its structure. Because it's geared around addressing a unique event, it follows a "General to Specific" pattern (which is how the majority of our adult education system is structured). You first remind the receiver about the time and place the event happened, then you describe the activities and behaviors, and then finally you invite the receiver to consider the results or response. It's a very logical flow, and you take the receiver on a descriptive journey with you as you go. You can check for understanding and recall as you go along, which means that the final message usually has a greater impact than if it was just presented without any supporting evidence.

Background

First, frame the discussion and then remind the receiver about the event which is to be discussed. For example:

> *"Marie, I want to talk to you about the e-mail that you sent to Jones and Brown this morning."*

> *"James, can I have five minutes with you to discuss the figures you submitted for this month's sales projection please."*

> *"Great, while we've got a few minutes without the rest of the team, I want to speak to you about what happened between you and Simon just before lunch."*

Activity

Now describe what specific activity or actions took place that need to be discussed and addressed. Remember the principles in *Chapter 1, Feedback Fundamentals*; describe what you noticed using your external senses without making any mind-reading statements or using any vague language! And remember that if you are quoting something that was said at the time, quote the phrase verbatim without adding or deleting anything. Arguing about exactly what was or wasn't said will only dilute the feedback message.

> *"When I opened your e-mail and read the content, I was rather surprised to see that you'd used the expression "your fault" to our second largest client."*

> *"As I was reviewing your submission to the Financial Controller, I noticed that the numbers in column D were out by a factor of 100."*

> *"When Simon offered his opinion on your presentation to the Executive Committee, I saw you lean forwards, raise your voice, and clench your fists while you addressed him."*

Results

Finally, highlight what happened as a result of the activity. If there were other people involved, talking about the response may be most appropriate. If not, a discussion around outcomes may be required. You then have a choice after this stage as to whether to be prescriptive and "tell" your team member something, or to make an enquiry and "ask" them something. This is the beginning of exploring the difference between being a **mentor** and sharing your experience, or being a **coach** and asking the receiver to reflect and draw their own conclusions. Mentoring and coaching are both essential ingredients for developing your new management skills, but both are subjects large enough to fill entire books on their own.

Tip

Make it a learning objective to become skilled at both mentoring and coaching.

To temporarily bridge the knowledge gap to becoming a skilled mentor or coach, consider the following question and answer:

> ➤ Q. What happens when a member of staff consistently relies on his or her manager to provide solutions to complex problems for them?
>
> A. When I've observed this in the past, staff miss out on the opportunity to innovate and develop their own critical thinking skills.

First I gave you an example of coaching, where I asked you to consider the question and conclude for yourself. Then, when I shared my experience in the answer, I switched to mentoring mode.

Here are two examples of how you can discuss results and then lead into a directive style of "telling" the person what to do or a non-directive style of "asking" them how they could do it differently:

"The result of your e-mail was a phone call to me from our client saying that they found your communication rude and unprofessional. This was a very unpleasant conversation for me and one that I don't want to have again. Next time you have to settle a difference of opinion with a large client, I want you to think about how the person will feel when they read what you have written."

"How do you think the senior partner felt when they read your e-mail saying it was their fault that we had failed to reach an agreement on a major point in the project? (wait for reply) How might that affect the recent tender we have submitted for a second bid?"

Essentially, you can stay in a directive and prescriptive mode of conversation whereby you use your own experience to give direction, or you can use a more non-directive, coaching style of conversation to encourage the receiver to make their own conclusions about where to go next. The choice is yours!

Tackling an uncomfortable subject

You can see that at this stage, no matter how new to management you are, you will have to tackle an uncomfortable conversation at some point when your team members do something that is morally or technically wrong, against company policy, or potentially dangerous to themselves or others, and therefore needs correcting. Depending on your personality and the behaviors of the person in question, this may cause some reluctance on your part to address it outright. The thing to understand is that the majority of people in the workplace don't enjoy difficult conversations either! So, you don't have to rejoice in it, but you do have to do it as a manager.

If any of this starts to ring true, keep the following principles in mind:

➤ Because a large portion of behavior is unconscious, sometimes people are genuinely unaware of their behaviors

➤ They can be even less aware of the *result* of their behaviors!

➤ You have a duty and a responsibility as a manager to direct, develop, and give feedback to your staff

➤ It's only by highlighting behaviors that need correcting that you can expect them to change

➤ A rotten tooth never gets better by itself, so only brush the teeth you want to keep…

The last point is somewhat tongue-in-cheek, however it represents a truism in the workplace; people will rarely correct their own behaviors unless it's pointed out, and if you leave situations unaddressed, they will deteriorate to the point of destruction. In my time, I've had to tackle people who constantly whinge about pay, conditions, department structure, the competence of the management, and so on. This generally has a negative impact on those around the whiner. I've also had to address people who regularly underperform and let their team members down, and even people who refuse to shower and wear deodorant! And you thought becoming a manager was all about your own office, car, private healthcare, and personalized stapler!

Consolidation exercise

By this stage of the book, you will have gained far more knowledge about giving feedback than most experienced managers have. The key is to consistently apply these techniques, and as you begin to notice the results, the steps you took to achieve them will become refined and ingrained skills. To highlight your progress so far, I have a small challenge for you.

Read the following examples of feedback and make some notes about whether the delivery is in keeping with what we've reviewed so far or whether there are areas for improvement:

1. "John, can I grab you for a second? I want to discuss the state that the treatment room was left in last night at the end of your shift. I noticed that you left a few minutes early last night and that there were still un-sterilized implements left out on the counter. I seem to remember that you completed a module on cross-infection in your last course—what was said on the course about leaving tools and equipment un-treated?"

2. "Julie, I want to give you some feedback about the way you conducted this morning's lesson. The children looked very puzzled and I don't think they understood what you were explaining. I wouldn't have put it across that way if I were teaching the class, and I don't think you were 100 percent clear about the key learning outcomes for that topic. Don't deliver it that way again please."

3. "Mike, I'm hearing some good things about the Westmoreland case. Carry on like that and I can see someone making Junior Partner pretty soon."

4. "Anya, can we discuss the audit process you ran for Bonds last week please? I spoke to their accountant and he remarked on how professional and thorough you were. It's really nice for me as your manager to hear feedback like that from our clients. He said you made everyone feel at ease and explained why you needed the documents you asked for. I'd encourage you to use the same tactic next week when you visit Blakemores, and please take Frankie with you, as I want her to pick up the techniques you use. That's exactly the sort of feedback that gets noticed by the board."

5. "Damian, I want to highlight something to you. When you served the young couple over by the door, you brought the main course while the young lady was still eating her starter. What effect do you think that had on their experience?"

Summary

In this chapter, you've learned an excellent feedback model that you can use to address specific performance issues. We've used examples of underperformance, but remember it can be used to highlight and re-enforce positive traits too. You also met Kate and read about the feedback I had early on in my career, and you have learned some more useful ways to deliver a feedback message. You've also had a chance to practice them yourself.

Take a few moments to reflect on what you have learned. Use the following questions as prompts:

➤ What is the most important message you need to deliver to one of your team to raise their performance?

➤ When will you deliver it?

➤ On a scale of 1 to 10, how committed are you to delivering it?

➤ What would move you up a notch if the number is anything less than 10?

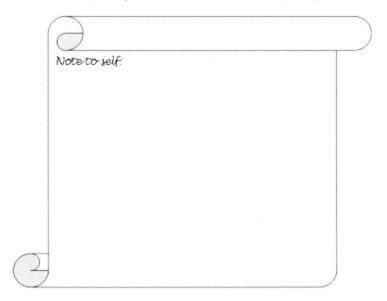

Note to self:

In the next chapter, you'll meet Trevor, and you'll also learn about the method I used to deliver a timekeeping reprimand when he continually tested my boundaries.

Tip

Before I leave you, can I give you a piece of feedback?

Remember when you opened this book today and started to read the chapter on the BAR model? I noticed that you worked diligently through the information and did each exercise fully. What effect do you think that has had on your skillset as a new manager in the department?

Imagine the positive effect on your staff when you put the entire book into practice!

Delivering a Reprimand

"Although what I am now to say is to be, in form, a reprimand, it is not intended to add a pang to what you have already suffered."

—Abraham Lincoln

Sometimes it's necessary to deliver a reprimand or "telling off" in the workplace because someone has violated the code of professional conduct, whether it's formalized or not. The issue could be as basic as someone not complying with a mandatory HR policy, or even being disrespectful or unprofessional. It's probably *the* most unpleasant conversation to have at work, and I hope it only comes around once in a blue moon for you. That being said, when it happens, it must be dealt with swiftly and effectively. And using the skills you'll learn in this chapter, you'll be able to do just that.

In this chapter you will:

➤ Meet Trevor, who just couldn't get to the office on time

➤ Learn three valuable lessons from my own painful experiences

➤ Learn how to apply the **DESC** feedback model

➤ Be able to turn back time and re-write a previous reprimand opportunity

Meet Trevor

I'm going to recount an experience now that illustrates the consequences of correcting someone's behavior when it gets out of line, but also what happens if you don't do it in a timely manner! It also exposes a source of conflict for managers everywhere.

Tip

There will be times in your new role when you may not agree with company policy, but as a manager, you will have to enforce it. *Act as if you fully support it.*

If you have to gripe about it then do it to your manager. In the long term, it will weaken your leadership position if you consistently take the approach of "The company says..." or "The MD wants us to...". Your people must work for *you* and they must see alignment between yours and the company's direction.

If you have anarchic tendencies, take the Frank Sinatra approach: leave and start your own business (I did it my way).

Trevor was exceptionally clever. I inherited him when I managed an established and well respected team, for which he was a team leader. He had many skills and good qualities—except timekeeping. Back then, we had rigid start and finish times and were required to be at our desks at a specific time and no later.

I noticed that Trevor consistently arrived at work 10 minutes later than the rest of the team, and I knew it had to be addressed. I hadn't had any management training at this stage, so I jumped in as best as I knew how. I called Trevor over to my desk and told him that I noticed that he was late getting in that morning, to which he commented that he had to visit the bathroom on the way into the office; this left me somewhat stunned and without an answer. While Trevor was regular in one sense, it wasn't the sort of regularity I was after.

On reflection, I suspect that this was a pre-prepared explanation, which you will find that people often carry around with them when they know they are bending the rules.

Trevor's timekeeping improved for a few days before slipping back into his old habit. With hindsight, I feel as if he was testing the boundaries to see how far he could push me, which will probably happen to you at some point too. (Trevor's retired now, but I hear he has trained a small army of rule breakers that he's left in his wake.)

The situation presented itself again and I felt compelled to act, but this time I made an even bigger mistake. At the end of our weekly team meeting, I looked everyone in the eye and told them that I expected them all to be in on time without exception. As you can imagine, this approach too had very little effect directly on Trevor, but it did upset the rest of the team.

Trevor strolled in late again and I called him straight over to my desk and told him that it wasn't acceptable for him to start later than everyone else and that he needed to be in on time. I was very frustrated and near to losing my temper. Trevor's reaction was quite peculiar; he told me all about the good work that he had been doing in the evenings that had saved the company time and money. I guess in his mind, the fact that he worked late justified him coming in later than everyone else. The minor detail he overlooked was that he was also getting paid overtime for working late! What a strange logic.

After that, he arrived at his desk right on time, but not a second earlier. I had corrected the situation but had made a few mistakes along the way, which had made it harder than necessary for me and the rest of the team. Let's review the learning from this:

My naïve approach	Your enlightened approach
I made an observation about an inappropriate behavior without specifying a correction.	Own your statement and say what you want the person to change.
I reprimanded the whole team for one person's behavior.	Directly address any issues with and only with the person concerned.
I allowed Trevor to give me a reason for breaking the rules.	When the situation calls for it, tell, don't ask. Check for understanding but don't get into a debate.

The DESC model

This is a great model to use when you need to strongly assert your opinion and where there's little room for negotiation, making it ideal for a reprimand.

Describe the situation

Like the **BAR** model introduced in *Chapter 3*, *Addressing Specific Performance Issues*, you will first give a summary of the event to be discussed. We already covered context setting in the previous chapter, so I'll use just one example here to illustrate this.

> *"Trevor, I want to talk to you about your timekeeping, and in particular the fact that you have been late three times this week."*

Express the impact

At this stage, you can state the wider effect that the observed behavior is having in the workplace—perhaps on other people, results, public relations, or some other area.

> *"When you turn up late, it makes the team appear unprofessional, and I'm concerned that it sets a bad example to the newer members of staff who are still fresh in their careers."*

State what you want to change

You can now give a positive and firm instruction as to how you want things to be different in the future. This is crucial after using a negative in the previous stage.

Tip

Bearing in mind the effect of language, ensure that the statements are about how to behave in future.

> *"I want you to be at your desk on time and ready to start work each day from here onwards."*

Communicate the consequences

Finally, it's important for the receiver to know that any deviation from what you have instructed will have undesirable side effects for them. And bear in mind that any sanctions that you state or intend to use must be carried out, or you will lose more than you are attempting to gain. Ever seen the parent of a small child threaten to take them home or take something away from them if they don't change what they are doing, only to see them not carry out the threat? Children and adults pick up on this; it's part of testing the boundaries.

> *"From now on, anything less than good time keeping will result in disciplinary proceedings. Do you understand?"*

Tip

Note how the very last part of the delivery is a closed question—one that invites a yes or no answer, not a discussion or debate.

If you find the receiver starts to debate the issue, simply re-state the last part again:

> *"Do you understand?"*

This is a short, sharp, shock approach, and it works very well.

Make a Note

A great advantage of the **DESC** model is that you can be effective without losing your temper, and losing your temper at work is rarely a good thing. Usually people lose their tempers when they've lost control of a situation and feel frustrated because of it. Things said in anger are often regretted, so stay in control of the situation and your feelings by dealing with them before they start to eat away at you.

Exercise – Could you have dealt better with a past reprimand?

As with all knowledge, the key to turning it into a repeatable skill is *practice*:

1. Cast your mind back and identify a time when you would like to have corrected someone's behavior but you didn't feel ready or equipped to do so.

2. With the incident in mind, work through each stage of the DESC model.

3. Using the following table, note down in the spaces what you would like to have said.

Tip

Obviously, written and spoken English are subtly different, but don't be too concerned about how it would sound if read out. The important thing is for you to internalize the structure of the model so that you can use it spontaneously when the need arises.

Describe the situation	
Express the impact	
State what you want to change	
Communicate the consequences	

Summary

In this chapter we have dealt with the less pleasant end of the feedback spectrum: delivering reprimands:

> ➤ I've shared some of my own experiences and some examples of how not to do it, using Trevor and the team as a case study
> ➤ You've picked up the **DESC** model, which is the last of the formal structures that I'm going to share with you in this book
> ➤ You've had a chance to put the **DESC** model into practice

It's time to reflect again, so here are a couple of thought provokers for you:

> ➤ How do you feel about delivering reprimands in the workplace?
> ➤ If you've ever been on the receiving end of one or have witnessed one, what impact did it have?
> ➤ If you've delivered one before, how well did it go?

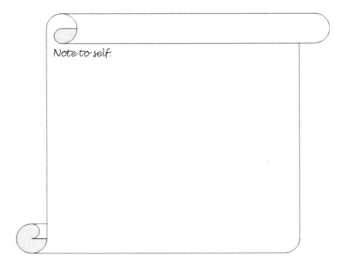

Note to self:

In the next chapter, we're going to deal with the tricky subject of giving feedback to someone who has violated your personal boundaries, even if they are more senior to you. Take a deep breath…

5

Giving Feedback to Colleagues and Managers

"I have nothing but respect for you–and not much of that."

—*Groucho Marx*

I once heard a CEO remark that he intended to be "Tough on the issue, not on the person." It didn't feel like it from where I was standing!

Perhaps a sharp word or thoughtless act has violated your personal boundaries at some point; the core values and principles that you hold most sacred were not respected and it left you feeling uncomfortable. A degree of this is inevitable in work and indeed life, and as a newly appointed manager, this isn't going to go away.

What will change, however, is that you will start to interact more with the upper levels of leadership in your organization–they tend to be the people with the strongest personalities. There may have been times when you walked away from a dialog feeling trampled upon, but if you previously felt unable to let the other person know that it wasn't okay, then rest assured that will change by the end of this section.

In this chapter you will:

> ➤ Meet Simon, who was both a source of inspiration and a challenge

> ➤ Learn to eloquently disagree with a senior member of staff on a technical issue

> ➤ Share your feelings when a conversation has left you feeling upset or disrespected

> ➤ Complete a multiple choice test that will fill you with feedback-giving confidence

Meet Simon

I once worked in an interim management position for a Senior Manager called Simon. The word I most associate with him is "sharp". He was very intelligent, quick thinking, and quick witted too—we shared many laughs together. He also was quite forthright with his opinions and could be quite blunt at times. These are all positive traits for management, except for one day when a comment he made just felt wrong. We were in a department tactics meeting with the rest of his first line; about six managers in total. I stated a view that must have been too controversial and he snapped quite quickly at me in front of the group. I felt embarrassed and didn't say much for the rest of the discussion. He didn't bring it up again, but it ate away at me inside.

This highlights a particular challenge in the workplace around maintaining your own self-esteem and status; sometimes people more senior than you will make comments that you won't want to respond to in the way that you would do if the conversation took place out of work. The language we use to describe the hierarchy in the workplace doesn't always help—we refer to Senior Leaders as being "higher up" or a "higher grade". This implies that you are lower than them. Psychologically, does this affect your self-esteem? Well the answer is "Only if you allow it to!" Always remember that someone else's grade within a company is a reflection of their past achievement and future potential; it has no bearing on your personal worth or right to be respected as an individual. And while some seniors will attempt to take advantage of this, it's your job to remain calm, confident, and assert your views appropriately.

Let's take a break now from my experiences with Simon and focus on building your skills in this area. The next few pages will contain strategies for you to use if and when you find yourself in a similar situation. I hope you appreciate the pain I went through when I learned these lessons, and if you promise to practice them diligently, then I promise to finish the story that I started and you can see how these techniques work in a heated setting!

Deflecting negative behaviors

One of my favorite stories that illustrate how to remain unaffected by other people's negativity comes from the teachings of the Buddha:

Make a Note

Buddha was walking through a village when an angry young man began insulting him. "You have no right teaching others," he said. "You are as stupid as everyone else. You are nothing but a fake." Buddha was not upset by these insults, instead he asked the young man, "Tell me, if you buy a gift for someone, and that person does not take it, to whom does the gift belong?" The man was surprised to be asked such a question and answered, "It would belong to me, because I bought the gift." The Buddha smiled and said, "That is correct. And it is exactly the same with your anger. If you become angry with me and I do not get insulted, then the anger falls back on you. You are then the only one who becomes unhappy, not me. All you have done is hurt yourself."

What this tells us is that ultimately, how we think, feel, and act is a personal choice. The challenge is when we don't get enough time to make a considered choice, such as being in the heat of an argument. The gap between stimulus and response isn't always long enough to choose the best response and we react emotionally, firing something back that we later regret, or say nothing and feel worse for not asserting ourselves in the moment. The topic of being assertive is vast and beyond the scope of this book; however, I would urge you to explore it as part of your ongoing personal development as a new manager.

Techniques for sensitive discussions

At times you will need to tread carefully when delivering feedback. Certain situations can quickly become volatile because of the personalities involved, or perhaps they are part of a wider and more passionate debate. Being direct and honest with your feedback doesn't absolve you of the responsibility to be diplomatic and respectful; remember that more eyes are on you as a manager as people expect you to be a role model in the department. I'm going to assume that I don't need to train you how to have a stand-up argument with someone, so instead we'll focus on some elegant and subtle techniques for getting your point across effectively when there's a more senior person and a keg of dynamite in the room with you.

Preframing the event

A **pre-frame** consists of the thoughts and feelings that you focus on about an event before you begin to deal with it. For example, if you have previously had cross words with someone in the past and need to debate an emotive issue with them in the future, you may feel anxious about the event. However, anxiety is often a feedback signal that you are paying attention to the wrong things, so pre-framing the event in a positive way in your mind will be more useful.

Here are three ways to positively pre-frame your feedback delivery:

➤ Think of the upcoming event as a learning opportunity that will make you stronger. There are very few people in life who feel no fear at all; courage is feeling afraid and taking action anyway.

➤ Imagine that your brain will be running 10 times faster than the spoken conversation (it is anyway) and reassure yourself that you have plenty of time to make a considered response that gets the best long term outcome.

➤ Visualize yourself walking away at the end. Imagine leaving behind anything unwanted or offensive that the recipient of your feedback said.

Building on these philosophies, let's look at some practical techniques now for delivering a feedback message to someone who's testing your boundaries.

Framing the conversation

Framing simply means to set an expectation about what is to be discussed. It acts as a sort of filter for the subject of the conversation. There are three types of frames that we can use to set up a delicate conversation.

Softening frames

These can be useful when you want to question something that has been said, but don't wish to appear too abrasive in your challenge. Maybe you think the idea is flawed or doesn't make sense but you want to probe gently at it without completely destroying the concept. Examples of a softening frame could be:

"Hmm... I'm curious about that, help me to understand..."

"I'm not sure I understood that correctly, how does..."

"Okay, let's play a scenario out, supposing that..."

Mismatch frames

Mismatch frames work well for certain individuals who are pre-disposed to arguing that black is white. I'm sure you've come across them in your career—whatever is said to them, they will always want to do the opposite and convert your thinking to theirs. Often this isn't a conscious pattern and they're not aware of it, it's just a habit they've formed. Mismatchers are contrary folk, so tell them they won't agree and they'll be more inclined to agree because they have to do the opposite!

So, for example, if you wanted agreement from someone with your idea about changing advertising agencies:

"Okay, you're not going to like this, but how about switching to another advertising agency?"

"I don't think you'll agree with this, but I wanted to get your view on switching ad agencies."

"I don't think this is going to fit with your plans, but I wanted to run it past you anyway...how would it fit if we switched away from our regular agency?"

Alternative frames

These are useful when you want to present a different viewpoint but perhaps tempers are running high or maybe it's just not appropriate to disagree outright. After someone has presented the idea that you wish to oppose, try employing some of the following approaches:

"I think that's a good idea, and I'd like to highlight an alternative..."

"That's a good possibility, and I think an alternative of XYZ has merit too if we explore it for a moment..."

"Yes that can definitely work, and I think we can also get there quicker by..."

Disagreeing with someone without them noticing

You may have noticed a particular word missing from the previous examples: "**but**". Linguistically, the word "but" has the effect of negating whatever argument was previously stated, making the other person defensive and making them expect an opposing position.

The word "and" acknowledges the previous argument and then builds on it gently with an alternative. Both words are grammatically interchangeable, so banish the word "but" for a while and practice using "and" instead. It maintains the rapport of the conversation and allows you to say the complete opposite with less resistance. "But" was used purposely in the examples about mismatch frames, *and* here we can leave it out.

Now I know that you're not yet convinced about the effectiveness of the aforementioned techniques, and you probably feel like they won't work in your organization. And I acknowledge that and I have an alternative viewpoint. My suggestion is that like everything else in this book, you test it out for yourself.

…See what I did there?

Sharing a feeling

The previous section was really focused on disagreeing with someone's opinion, maybe on a technical point or a strategic plan. This was mostly based on logic, with not much said about emotions. This section deals with the feelings you are left with when tempers have been frayed or you feel disrespected.

I'm going to start by reminding you of one of the core principles that we covered in *Chapter 1, Feedback Fundamentals*—being honest. Again, you should choose your time and place wisely, but telling someone exactly how you feel is immensely powerful. Of course, this is practically impossible for anyone who is male, was raised by parents who were educated in post-Victorian Britain, or who had a boarding school education. I'm being facetious here, but I do understand that talking about feelings doesn't come naturally to everyone. However, it's worth the investment in effort to come to terms with verbalizing your feelings at an appropriate time and place. This isn't a book on therapy, but there's a reason that "Talking Cures" are so popular.

Follow these steps for success with sharing a feeling:

1. Tell the person that you want to speak to them in private about something that they have said or done.
2. Remind them of the specific situation in which the event occurred.
3. Repeat what they said or describe what they did at the time.
4. Express how you felt after this.

Tip

Notice that I've resisted using the words "How they *made* you feel" as I believe in taking responsibility for your own thoughts and feelings; of course, your overall state is the sum total of your thoughts, feelings, and sensory inputs, so describe your emotions and own them. You can't always stop waves from appearing in the ocean, but you can choose which ones to surf.

Sharing my feelings with Simon

Fortunately, the week after the aforementioned incident, he and I had an hour alone in his office. We discussed various other matters, and then at the end of the session, I told him that I needed to speak to him about what went on in last week's meeting. I reminded him of what had been said, and then I told him that I felt berated in front of my colleagues. This had a rather unexpected effect; he coughed, shifted in his seat, and told me that he had been feeling rather stressed recently and had been suffering from chest pains. He apologized for what he'd said and it was never brought up again.

Now it wasn't the last time that he and I had a heated exchange, but it taught me the power of sharing the feeling I was left with, and in a strange way allowed me to let it go and move on. The frustration I had felt at the time of not asserting myself in the moment had gone, and Simon knew that he had crossed a boundary. While your manager has a responsibility to train and develop you, sometimes you have to remind them how to behave too.

I've given you strategies in this chapter to deal with situations where you need to deflect negativity, proceed sensitively, disagree subtly, and share a feeling; perhaps due to the environment you are in or because of the seniority of the other person. You should now have plenty of resources at hand to handle the majority of challenging conversations for now, although remember that working cultures are made up of many people, all of whom are different. Some seniors like to have a stand-up row with their staff and respect them for it afterwards, so it is possible to go head to head with someone and still have a positive outcome. What I've focused on here is how to disagree diplomatically and subtly and how to express how you may be feeling after some sharp words. I've found these to be crucial skills to have as a newly appointed manager while you are still finding your feet in the role and are in effect testing other people's boundaries while your own are being stretched too!

Quiz: Chapters 1 to 5

The following quiz aims to consolidate all of your learning so far throughout the book. You've learned seven key principles, three useful models, and dozens of other tips and techniques along the way. To keep that learning fresh, we're going to re-activate it now with a multiple choice quiz. (Check your answers in the Appendix!)

Q1. A member of staff plays a dangerous prank in the work environment and endangers some colleagues. Which feedback model would best fit the situation and why?

1. WIN
2. BAR
3. DESC
4. STAR

Q2. In the EARSHOT principles, "S" stands for:

1. Standard
2. Specific
3. Short
4. Situation

Q3. While giving a presentation to a client, a team member makes a small error that they were unaware of, but could improve on next time. Do you:

1. Take five minutes in private after the presentation to discuss it.
2. Stop them immediately and correct them.
3. Discuss it at the next team meeting.

Q4. A Senior Leader remarks that one of your team has attitude issues. Do you:

1. Pass the remark on directly at the next opportunity.
2. Ask for some specific examples of behavior to clarify the remark.
3. Challenge it and defend your member of staff without accepting it.

Q5. A member of your team uses an incorrect technical term in a document, but you spot it before it is released. They are usually diligent and accurate. Do you:

1. Make a note of it in their file to use in pay award discussions.
2. Reprimand them severely and state the consequences of what could have happened.
3. Highlight the error and emphasize the correct terminology to use in future.

Q6. It is time to deliver a performance appraisal. In preparing your feedback, do you:

1. Consider recent performance as people are only as good as their last job.
2. Use the BAR model to positively discuss this quarter's successes.
3. Use the WIN model to deliver balanced and considered feedback from the year.

Q7. You are in a team meeting discussing budget cuts and your immediate manager becomes agitated and shouts at you in front of the team to find some savings or get a new job. You feel embarrassed. Do you:

1. Say nothing and double your cost saving efforts.
2. Ask them to step outside for a moment and shout back.
3. Talk to them in private about the impact of the comment and ask that they maintain an adult and civil tone.

Q8. One of your team is consistently missing their performance targets, although they are a pleasant and helpful member of the team. Do you:

1. Overlook the issue to spare their feelings as they are a popular member of the team.

2. Using evidence of results, ask how they could reach the required performance.

3. Encourage them to consider a sideways move to another area.

Q9. A colleague has been classified as an underperformer in the performance management system and believes it to be unfair. They ask your opinion. Do you:

1. Highlight examples of how they perform, asking how it might be perceived by others.

2. Tell them that you don't think this year has been their best year.

3. Be honest with your opinion about why they have been ranked lowly.

Q10. You have a team member who is very strong technically but is prone to making offensive remarks to the opposite sex. Do you:

1. Use the DESC model in private the very next time it happens.

2. Use the WIN model to discuss their positive traits but emphasize areas for improvement too.

3. Compile a list of incidents and pass them to HR to deal with officially.

Summary

In this chapter, we've looked at feedback conversations that can be particularly difficult due to the seniority of the other person involved. You've taken some wisdom from Gautama Buddha and applied it to your own thinking about responding to abrasive situations. You've learned techniques for disagreeing eloquently with your boss, and you've discovered the power of sharing your feelings with someone. You also met Simon and completed a multiple choice quiz to consolidate your learning so far.

Thinking back over what you've read:

> ➤ What has this chapter evoked for you personally?

> ➤ Where would this approach have been useful for you?

> ➤ Which feelings most challenge you in this area?

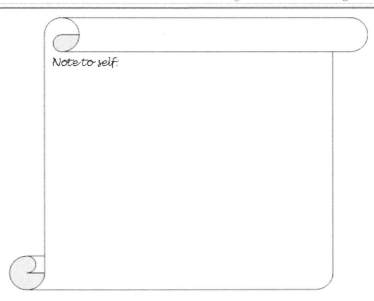

Note to self:

In the next chapter, we will pull all of the previous material together and add some extra techniques to make you a model of feedback excellence.

We're nearly at the end…and also the beginning.

6

Integrating Your New Skills

"I don't go for perfect, I go for excellent. The way to become excellent is through practice."

—*Robert Kiyosaki*

We've covered a huge amount of information in this short book. There's enough material in here to put you way ahead of your colleagues in how you deliver feedback, and when you take the ideas and implement them, your staff's performance will begin to climb steadily.

In this chapter you'll:

- ➤ Improve the delivery of your feedback
- ➤ Learn the single most important four-step plan that I've ever seen and apply it to feedback sessions
- ➤ Finish the book with an action plan to get you started on becoming the manager who gives the best feedback in your entire company!

Improving your delivery

Much of this book has focused around the use of language. I've given you structures and patterns for how to shape what you say—**syntax**—and I've also emphasized the use or non-use of certain words and phrases that affect how your message is received—**semantics**. Let's now explore another topic area that can affect the impact that your feedback has; your **emotional state**. By this I mean the sum total of how you are thinking, feeling, and behaving at the time that you have your conversation. Your emotional state is probably the biggest performance driver for any endeavor that you carry out, so it makes sense to ensure that it's a positive and focused one. If you've ever watched a tennis player just before match point, a football player before a penalty kick, or a boxer enter the ring, you'll notice that they are in a very focused and determined state just before the critical moment.

Athletic performance requires certain states of mind that have some similarities with the world of work. Imagine the way that your message could be affected by you feeling any of these emotions in either situation:

➤ Angry

➤ Upset

➤ Nervous

➤ Distracted

➤ Confused

➤ Anxious

➤ Frustrated

➤ Sad

➤ Fearful

➤ Irritable

So just like an athlete, before you engage in a feedback conversation, please take a moment to take stock of how you are feeling and whether you are in the optimum mental state to have a critical conversation. Whatever emotion you find yourself feeling before the conversation is likely to be related to the conversation you are about to have. Feelings, after all, are a feedback mechanism on your thoughts and actions; they let you know whether something fits with your personal values or not. If you are feeling anything less than a calm and confident state, use the following sequence to manage it:

1. Identify the feeling. Are you anxious, afraid, or annoyed, for example?

2. Acknowledge the feeling, remind yourself that it's okay to feel this way, and that the feeling has a purpose.

3. Ask yourself exactly what the purpose is of that feeling and what you need to pay attention to in order for the feeling to change.

You can run through this sequence in your head in less than a minute, and nobody else needs to know what answers you came up with.

Tip

Anxiety, for example, is often a feedback signal that you are focusing on the wrong things. Going back to the example we used earlier in the book, a tight-rope walker would understandably be feeling anxious if they were just to focus on how badly they could be injured if they fell. Not surprising really!

If you find yourself feeling a specific way about what has happened just before you are due to have your conversation, then changing your physical posture is also an effective way of changing your emotional state and throwing off the residue from the day's events. Getting up from your seat and taking a quick walk, preferably outside the building, has a noticeable effect on how you feel. If that's not possible, just standing up, stretching, and breathing deeper than normal will change the way that you feel in the moment.

If you are demanding peak performance from your staff, don't you owe it to them to put yourself in the best possible performance state too?

Have I:

➤ Recalled as many facts as possible that are relevant to the issue?

➤ Chosen a suitable model or approach?

➤ Selected an appropriate time and place?

➤ Prepared myself mentally and emotionally?

If the answer to all of these is "yes", you need to begin!

A four-step plan to achieve just about anything

1. Decide on the outcome you want.
2. Choose a course of action.
3. Pay attention to what happens in the moment.
4. Change course if necessary.

Using these four steps will get you a long way in life in many different situations, and for the purposes of developing your feedback skills, let's look at how it relates to giving feedback messages.

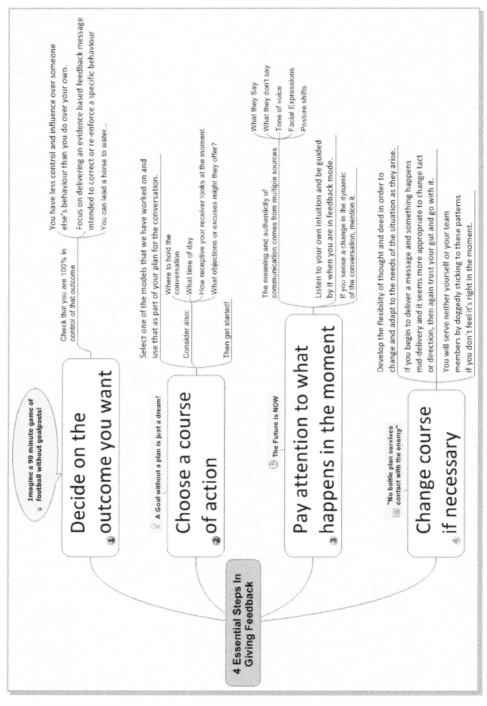

Here's an example of how the four-tep plan could relate to a workplace feedback conversation:

1. Decide on the outcome you want.

    To raise the awareness of Jane's behavior in team meetings to Jane and to ensure that she understands that change is necessary.

2. Choose a course of action.

    Book a private one-to-one meeting with Jane directly after the team meeting. Use the **BAR** model to structure the conversation.

3. Pay attention to what happens in the moment.

    Notice how Jane reacts during the conversation and listen to what underlying reasons she offers for her behavior.

4. Change course if necessary.

    Be prepared to abandon the model and pursue an alternative line of enquiry if you think that Jane is about to air a deeper issue and that the time will be better spent discussing something that will leverage a more impactful change within Jane. It's never in anyone's interests to doggedly finish a pattern or technique if you suddenly notice something more significant to pursue.

How to balance feedback with encouragement

Throughout these chapters, I've stressed the importance of speaking in specific, behavioral terms that help people raise their performance. And while it's a crucial skill to learn as a new manager, I want to add that people still expect and value the human touch in the workplace. So it isn't my intention to turn you into an observational android who's devoid of warmth and character; rather to equip you with the flexibility and choice of response that best suits the situation. It was Albert Einstein who said:

> *"It would be possible to describe everything scientifically, but it would make no sense; it would be without meaning, as if you described a Beethoven symphony as a variation of wave pressure."*

Tip
So remember, people will still benefit from you casually saying "well done", "good work", and "great job" around the office!

Praise is a terrific motivator, and you should use it when it's appropriate to let people know that you notice and value their contribution. Most often, people don't leave because of the job, they leave because of the manager! So, let your people know that you appreciate them by telling them, praising them, and even buying them doughnuts if that's the culture in your office (somehow a light salad and a mineral water just doesn't say it like 350 calories of trans fat in partially hydrogenated vegetable oil).

And while we're on the subject, I'll say well done to you for reading and completing the exercises in this book. Given that management is a profession, you'd be surprised how few people actually invest in their own development once they have the title. We used to joke in Karate class that the Brown Belts were sharper and meaner than some of the Black Belts—they were hungrier for promotion at that stage, and the complacency of having "arrived" hadn't set in. So even before you master these feedback skills, you'll be ahead of most of the management population by simply becoming aware of these principles and techniques.

Action plan

From here onwards, it's all down to you; I can take you no further. I'm going to invite you to reflect on what you've learned and then commit to putting these skills into practice regularly over the coming weeks and months. Take some time to complete the following questions:

The thing that I will use most from this book is:
The thing that I haven't yet realized a use for is:
My biggest challenge will be to:
The reason I'm committed to overcoming it is because when I do:
The piece of feedback that I most need to deliver is to _____ and is about:
The specific next steps for me are: Date:

Summary

In this final chapter of the book you have:

- ➤ Learned the importance of getting going, and not being perfect
- ➤ Realized the importance of your emotional state when engaging in feedback
- ➤ Seen the four key steps to achieving feedback mastery
- ➤ Reviewed the importance of praise and encouragement
- ➤ Committed to an action plan that will take your feedback skills to a level that will surprise your staff, your manager, and yourself

What's important from here is that you make a start on your feedback journey; wherever you are starting from is fine. You may be waiting to take up your new management role and want to learn some new skills before beginning. Perhaps you are still within your first few months of promotion and have read this book because of a challenging situation you've had. Or maybe you are an experienced manager who enjoys learning and developing new skills. Whatever stage of your career you are at, the important thing to understand is that personal and professional development is a journey, not a destination, and in some respects, we are all still a "work in progress". There will always be scope to do something bigger, better, or faster, so consider these lessons as things to take with you along the way. Don't expect everything to be perfect the first time you put it into practice; it's okay to experiment and learn from whatever results you get, even if conversations and situations don't go the way you planned.

Bear in mind also that people get promoted into management for a variety of reasons. Ideally you'll be a strong player in all areas of your work with the right set of personal attributes too. In reality, some individuals make it into management because they are very assertive and telling people what to do comes easily. Others are highly intelligent and can solve problems easily. And then others are very successful at their current roles and outperform their peers in delivering work on time, to budget, and to a high quality. Depending on your own strengths and needs, some parts of giving feedback will come easier to you than other parts. So the aim for now isn't to get it all perfect to begin with, it's simply to begin.

Good luck in your new role!

> Appendix

Chapter 1 – "Where are you now?" answers

1. False
2. False
3. True
4. True
5. False
6. True
7. False
8. True
9. True
10. False

Chapter 3 – Consolidation exercise answers

1. This is an example of the BAR model, whereby the background is described, then the activity that took place and finally the feedback receiver is asked an open question to encourage them to reflect on the results of the incident.

2. This paragraph contains multiple mind-reads whereby the giver attempts to guess what the children were thinking and feeling. The giver also uses a negative instruction at the end, saying what not to do, but without any positive guidance about how it could be better.

3. This is an interesting example; it isn't particularly useful feedback as it's very vague and doesn't contain any specific references to behaviors that can be repeated and strengthened. It does, however, serve well as motivational praise and for this reason has its place in a manager's vocabulary. Be clear, however, that this is a general "pat on the back", to be used as reward and acknowledgment as opposed to a development conversation.

4. This again is an example of the BAR model in practice and this time, the manager shares their positive feelings about the event during the feedback delivery. Although there are elements of a third-party being involved, the manager puts them across in a factual way as supporting evidence. While these models are useful structures to assist you in getting started, your mission is to use them as naturally as you can in conversation. Principles are more important than rigid structures.

5. This is an example of using the BAR model with an inquiry to the receiver at the end, to consider the effects of their actions. It uses a coaching style of delivery and is a good example of how coaching can be applied "in the moment" to good effect, outside of a formal coaching conversation.

Chapter 5 – Chapters 1 to 5 quiz answers

1. C: The incident involves someone's personal safety being compromised and as such, has to be corrected swiftly. There is little value on reflecting on other aspects of performance such as successes and learnings; this is a discipline related conversation and is best delivered succinctly and to the point.

2. B

3. A

4. B

5. C

6. C

7. C

8. B

9. A

10. A

www.ingramcontent.com/pod-product-compliance
Lightning Source LLC
LaVergne TN
LVHW081348050326
832903LV00024B/1366